Surviving a Hurricane

by Heather Adamson

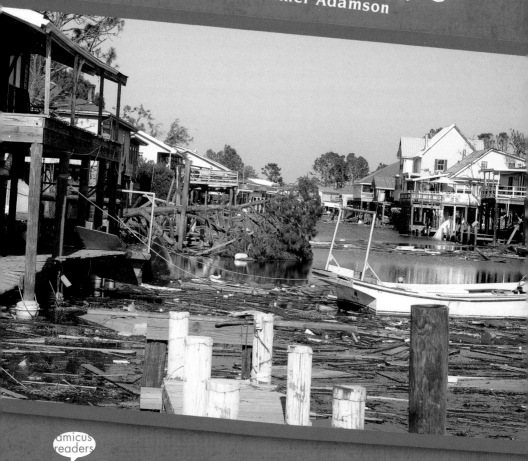

amicus readers

2

Say hello to amicus readers.

You'll find our helpful dog, Amicus, chasing a ball—to let you know the reading level of a book.

A

Learn to Read
Frequent repetition of sentence structures, high frequency words, and familiar topics provide ample support for brand new readers. Approximately 100 words.

1

Read Independently
Repetition is mixed with varied sentence structures and 6 to 8 content words per book are introduced with photo label and picture glossary supports. Approximately 150 words.

2

Read to Know More
These books feature a higher text load with additional nonfiction features such as more photos, time lines, and text divided into sections. Approximately 250 words.

Amicus Readers are published by Amicus
P.O. Box 1329, Mankato, Minnesota 56002
www.amicuspublishing.us

Printed in the United States of America at at Corporate Graphics, in North Mankato, Minnesota.

Series Editor   Rebecca Glaser
Series Designer   Bobbi J. Wyss
Photo Researcher   Heather Dreisbach

Library of Congress Cataloging-in-Publication Data
Adamson, Heather, 1974-
Surviving a hurricane / by Heather Adamson.
   p. cm. – (Amicus Readers. Be prepared)
Includes index.
Summary: "Discusses the dangers of hurricanes, how to prepare for them, and how to stay safe during and after a hurricane"–Provided by publisher.
ISBN 978-1-60753-151-7 (library binding)
1. Hurricanes–Juvenile literature. 2. Hurricanes–Safety measures–Juvenile literature. I. Title.
QC944.2.A325 2012
613.6'9–dc22
                                                    2010042154

Photo Credits
Planet Observer/Universal Images Group/Getty Images, Cover; Doug Webb/Alamy, 1; Worldspec/NASA/Alamy, 5; Kevin Howchin/Alamy, 6, 21bm; Stephen Frink/Getty Images, 7; Joe Raedle/Getty Images, 9, 20b; Jim Reed/Getty Images, 10; Stephen Morton/Getty Images, 11; kzenon/iStockphoto, 12; STAN HONDA/AFP/Getty Images, 13, 20m; OMAR TORRES/AFP/Getty Images, 15; Steven Clevenger/Getty Images, 17; Scott Olson/Getty Images, 19, 20t; Moses1978/Dreamstime.com, 21t; dmac/Alamy, 21tm; Donald Gruener/iStockphoto, 21b; newphotoservice/Shutterstock, 22a; ILYA AKINSHIN/Shutterstock, 22b; Mihalec/Dreamstime.com, 22c; Timmary/Shutterstock, 22d

1035   3-2011
10 9 8 7 6 5 4 3 2 1

Table of Contents

Hurricanes

Hurricanes are **tropical storms** that form in the ocean. Storm clouds circle around a calm spot called an eye. The giant storm spins to shore.

If you live near an ocean, you should be prepared.

tropical storm

storm surge

Hurricanes are dangerous when they hit land. High waves called **storm surges** crash into things. Rain floods roads and homes. The twisty clouds can form tornadoes and break windows and walls.

Preparing for a Hurricane

Scientists can **forecast** hurricanes before they hit land.

A **hurricane watch** means that a hurricane may come to your area within 48 hours.

forecast

A **hurricane warning** means that a hurricane is likely within 36 hours.

Cover the windows with shutters or boards. Then tie down or put away outside things that might blow away.

Hurricanes can knock out power and water for several days. Your family needs supplies to be ready. Make sure you have food, water, and a radio in your storm kit.

Your family may decide to **evacuate**. This means you must leave your home. You can stay at a shelter or with friends in a safe place away from the ocean.

During a Hurricane

If you don't leave the city, go to a shelter before the hurricane hits. Stay inside until the storm is over.

If your family stays at home, get in a small room with no windows. You do not want to get hurt from flying glass.

After a Hurricane

Flooding can make water from faucets unsafe. It may be dirty and can make you sick.

Use the water from your storm supplies until it is safe again.

S. Claiborne Av

Rain can stay for days after a hurricane. And the power can be out even longer. Play inside until the weather clears.

You can help clear branches and **debris** when the sun shines again.

debris

Photo Glossary

debris
broken glass, pieces of trash, or damaged trees from a storm

evacuate
to leave an area that is unsafe

forecast
to predict or guess where a storm may hit

hurricane warning
an announcement that hurricane winds are expected within 36 hours; red flags tell ships to come in.

hurricane watch
an announcement that hurricane level winds are possible within 48 hours

storm surge
walls of water that come from waves and high water of the ocean

tropical storm
a windy storm that forms in warmer areas of the oceans

Activity: Make a Hurricane Model

Try making this model to see how hurricanes work.

What You Need:

Bowl of water

Spoon

Paperclip and string

1. Tie the paperclip to the string. Stir the water quickly in circles to make it swirl.

2. Hang the paperclip in the water near one side of the bowl, then the other. What happens?

3. Hang the paperclip in the middle of the swirl. What happens?

On the sides of the bowl, the paperclip will be pushed out in the direction of the swirling water. In the middle, the paperclip will stay calm in the "eye" of the storm. Hurricane winds work the same way. They blow large objects in all directions.

Ideas for Parents and Teachers

Be Prepared, an Amicus Readers Level 2 series, provides simple explanations of what storms are and offers reassuring steps that kids and families can take to be prepared for disasters. As you read this book with your children or students, use the ideas below to help them get even more out of their reading experience.

Before Reading

* Read the title and ask the students if they've ever experienced a hurricane or know someone who has.

* Ask the students what they think the difference between a hurricane and other storms is. Ask them why we need to be prepared for hurricanes.

* Use the photo glossary words to help them predict what they will learn from the book.

Read the Book

* Ask the students to read the book independently.

* Provide support where necessary. Point out that the photo labels can help them learn new words.

After Reading

* Ask the students to retell what they learned about hurricanes and how to prepare for them. Compare their answers to what they said before reading the book.

* Have students do the activity on page 22.

Index

Web Sites

Fema for Kids: Hurricanes
http://www.fema.gov/kids/hurr.htm

Hurricane Survival for Kids: What Do You Do?
http://www.unctv.org/hurricane/kids02.html

Weather Wiz Kids: Hurricanes
http://www.weatherwizkids.com/weather-hurricane.htm

Web Weather for Kids: Hurricanes
http://eo.ucar.edu/webweather/hurricanehome.html